International Cooking Collection

Good Fast Food

International
Cooking Collection

Good Fast Food

Clare Gordon-Smith

CONTENTS

Published exclusively for Cupress (Canada) Ltd
20 Torbay Road, Markham, Ontario L3R 1G6, Canada
by Woodhead-Faulkner (Publishers) Ltd, Simon & Schuster International Group

This edition first published 1988
© Woodhead-Faulkner (Publishers) Ltd 1988
All rights reserved
ISBN 0-920691-66-8
Printed and bound in Italy

INTRODUCTION

With today's busy lifestyle there must be occasions when you just don't have time to prepare a meal.

It may be that you don't want to spend time in the kitchen and you would rather be in the garden on a hot summer's day, or relaxing with family and friends at weekends or after a long day at work.

Or else you've spent all day at work and decide to ask friends over for supper. What can you give them when you have to shop and produce a meal in a couple of hours and you prefer to show off your cooking skills rather than serve a ready-prepared, additive-packed convenience meal?

If this sounds familiar then read on, this book is for you! There is no need to grab a snack or take-out morning, noon and night, ending up with a badly-balanced diet because you lead a hectic lifestyle. All the recipes in this book take no longer than 20 minutes to prepare and a maximum of 30 minutes to cook, with many taking a lot less. The cooking is done on the burner or broiled, though many recipes involve no cooking at all.

Here you will find quick but healthy solutions to entertaining and lunch and supper dishes along with delicious desserts that take less than 15 minutes to make. And if you find cooking for one more trouble than it's worth, or never find time to consider breakfast, then turn to the section on instant alternatives: some of these recipes serve one or two and they are all light and nourishing —especially suitable for breakfast as they can be prepared in under 5 minutes.

BASIC ESSENTIALS

To obtain food that is both quick to prepare and healthy you need a well-stocked refrigerator and store cupboard. Your refrigerator should contain eggs, milk, butter, curd cheese or farmer's cheese, cottage or cream cheese, hard cheese, bacon and ham, mayonnaise, plain yogurt, fruit juices, lemon and fresh herbs. A good idea is to grow your own herbs so that they can be picked when needed.

A small freezer is useful for bread, frozen vegetables and fruit, fresh pasta (which can be cooked from frozen), a few chicken joints and lamb chops, ice creams and desserts which can be used from frozen. Frozen heavy cream can also be most useful, especially when friends drop in unexpectedly.

A well-stocked store cupboard should have a good selection of the following non-perishable, very useful items.

- Canned tomatoes—usually cheaper, and quicker to prepare than fresh when you need peeled tomatoes. Now available ready-chopped.
- A can of tuna to mix with pastas, salads and sauces. Canned crab, salmon, mackerel, sardine fillets and anchovies are also good standbys.
- Canned beans, e.g. lima beans, kidney beans, chili beans, navy beans and garbanzo beans.

•Various canned fruits, in syrup or natural fruit juice—good for both sweet and savory sauces and instant desserts.

•A package of dried breadcrumbs—for coating and binding food.

•A good selection of dried fruit and nuts. You can now buy dried apricots which need no pre-soaking. Nuts are especially useful for garnishes and decorations. Filberts are available ready chopped and roasted in bags—ideal for adding crunch and flavor to many dishes.

•A selection of bouillon cubes to flavor soups and sauces. These can now be bought specifically for fish, vegetables, chicken, lamb and beef. Cans of consommé are also very good for stocks.

•A selection of oils—very important for flavor, e.g. olive oil for dressings —buy virgin olive oil as this has the best flavor. Sunflower oil is particularly good for frying and also for some dressings.

•A selection of vinegars, such as red and white wine vinegar and a few flavored ones—e.g. cider vinegar, tarragon vinegar and raspberry vinegar.

•A range of mustards, including smooth and coarse-grain. Horseradish is also good for flavor.

•A selection of dried herbs—to use when fresh are unobtainable. Thyme, marjoram, oregano, bay leaves and basil are good ones to have.

•Spices are also important, e.g. chili powder, ground red pepper, ground coriander, ground cumin and garam masala. Also have garlic powder handy.

•Pre-cooked rice, instant mashed potatoes, commercially made custard, sponge rings and meringue nests are also useful to have, when you haven't got time to make your own.

Certain items of equipment will also help speed up many of the preparation and cooking processes. A food processor will rapidly chop onions and herbs, slice vegetables, grate cheese, prepare breadcrumbs, make purees, and blend soups, patés and drinks. You may wish to make breadcrumbs and grated cheese in bulk and store them in the freezer. They can be used straight from frozen—thawing is unnecessary.

Certain items of small equipment are also invaluable when time is short, for instance a good sharp French cook's knife and a large chopping board, a selection of heavy-based saucepans, a frying pan, a few wooden spoons, and a balloon whip. Always have a few screw-top jars at hand—these are ideal for combining ingredients for salad dressings.

A microwave oven is especially useful for defrosting those standbys you have tucked away in the freezer e.g. bread, and portions of chicken and other meat. Of course you may be able to speed up the cooking or preparation processes even more with a microwave oven. The cooking times for the recipes in this book are already short, but you may wish to cut these down even more by consulting your microwave handbook. A microwave oven is also ideal for cooking vegetable accompaniments and for carrying out countless preparation tasks, such as softening butter, melting chocolate or heating small quantities of water.

ENTERTAINING MENUS

Sometimes it can take almost as long to plan a menu as to cook the entire meal—below are some menu suggestions to help you. In each menu at least one of the courses can be prepared or partly prepared in advance. Many of the desserts and salads may be prepared and then placed in the refrigerator until required. Soups may be made in advance omitting any cream or yogurt—heat through when required, stirring in the cream or yogurt at the end.

Serves 2
Avocado with Herb Dressing
Pheasant with Plum Sauce
Fresh Fruit Selection and
Cheeseboard

Serves 4
Roulades of Salmon, Spinach
and Lemon Sole
Apple-Tossed Veal
Summer Fruit Salad

Serves 4
Mussel Salad
Honey-Glazed Game Hens
Fruit Melba

Serves 4
Cream of Pea Soup
Lamb with Cranberry Sauce
Zabaglione

Serves 4
Mussel and Saffron Soup
Duck Breasts in Orange Sauce
Cherries in Red Wine

Serves 4
Cream of Watercress Soup
Venison with Spiced Cherry Sauce
Chestnut Pavlovas

NOTES

All spoon measurements are level.

Use U.S. grade large eggs unless otherwise stated.

Freshly ground black pepper is intended where pepper is listed.

Fresh herbs are used unless otherwise stated. If unobtainable, dried herbs can be substituted in cooked dishes but halve the quantities.

TOMATO PASTA SHELLS

1 tablespoon sunflower oil
1 onion, chopped
1 clove garlic, crushed
  (optional)
14 oz can chopped
  tomatoes
1/3 lb mushrooms, sliced
1 yellow pepper, cored,
  seeded and chopped

3 zucchini, sliced
1 teaspoon dried oregano
1 tablespoon chopped
  parsley
1 teaspoon sugar
1 teaspoon wine vinegar
4 cups fresh pasta shells
1 tablespoon chopped
  parsley to garnish

Serves 4
Preparation time:
10 minutes
Cooking time:
15–20 minutes
Freezing:
Recommended for
sauce only

1. Heat the oil in a pan, add the onion and saute until soft. Add the remaining ingredients, except the pasta, bring to the boil, then simmer for 15–20 minutes.
2. Meanwhile, cook the pasta according to package instructions. Drain thoroughly, add to the sauce and toss well.
3. Serve immediately, sprinkled with the parsley.

HAM WITH APPLE RINGS

2 tablespoons butter
2 teaspoons sunflower oil
1 tablespoon prepared
  mustard
2 dessert apples, cored and
  cut into rings

2 tablespoons chopped
  sage (optional)
4 ham steaks, 1/2 inch
  thick
parsley or sage leaves to
  garnish

Serves 4
Preparation time:
7 minutes
Cooking time:
4–5 minutes
Freezing:
Not recommended

1. Heat the butter and oil in a frying pan, add the mustard, apple, and sage if using, and saute gently while cooking the ham.
2. Broil the ham steaks for 4–5 minutes, turning once.
3. Arrange the ham on warmed serving plates and top with the apple rings. Garnish with parsley or sage to serve.

VARIATION
Replace the apple with peaches, pineapple or pears.

SAVORY MUFFINS

Several types of muffin are now available, so use your favorite for this recipe. Children will find this a yummy after-school snack.

6 raisin and bran muffins
¼ cup butter
6 slices ham, cut in half
1½ tablespoons mild
* mustard*

8 oz hard cheese,
* e.g. Cheddar or*
* Wensleydale, sliced*
* thinly*
tomato slices and parsley
* sprigs to garnish*

Serves 4–6
Preparation time:
5 minutes
Cooking time:
3–5 minutes
Freezing:
Not recommended

1. Split and toast the muffins and spread with the butter.
2. Place a piece of ham on each muffin half and spread with a little mustard. Top with the cheese.
3. Broil for about 3 minutes, until the cheese has melted.
4. Garnish with tomato and parsley to serve.

CHEESE AND TOMATO OMELET

Omelets make a quick substantial meal. Any leftovers you have can be used as flavorings.

2 tablespoons chopped
* parsley*
1 tablespoon water
4 eggs, beaten
2 tablespoons butter
2 tomatoes, chopped

¾ cup grated Cheddar
* cheese*
salt and pepper to taste
Belgium endive leaves
* and cucumber slices*
* to garnish*

Serves 2
Preparation time:
5 minutes
Cooking time:
5 minutes
Freezing:
Not recommended

1. Beat the parsley, water, and salt and pepper into the eggs.
2. Melt the butter in an omelet pan and, when foaming, add the egg mixture. Cook over a low heat for about 3 minutes, until just beginning to set. Add the tomatoes and cheese and cook for 1–2 minutes.
3. Fold the omelet over and serve immediately, garnished with Belgium endive and cucumber.

VARIATIONS

Add any of the following: 1 cup sliced mushrooms, ¾ cup shredded ham, ¾ cup diced cooked chicken, 1 diced green or red pepper, 2 small cooked sliced potatoes.

HERBY LIVER AND BACON

3 tablespoons all-purpose
*   flour*
2 teaspoons dried thyme
2 tablespoons chopped
*   parsley*
1 lb calves' or lambs' liver,
*   sliced and cut into strips*

¼ cup sweet butter
6 bacon strips, chopped
3 tomatoes, chopped
salt and pepper to taste
parsley sprigs to garnish

1. Mix the flour with the herbs, and salt and pepper and use to coat the liver.
2. Melt the butter in a pan until foaming, add the liver and bacon and fry for 5–7 minutes until tender, stirring in the tomato after 3 minutes.
3. Serve garnished with parsley.

Serves 4
Preparation time:
10 minutes
Cooking time:
5–7 minutes
Freezing:
Not recommended

VEGETABLE PIZZA

Pizzas are traditionally made on an uncooked dough base.
To speed up the process, I have used French bread.

1 tablespoon sunflower oil	*¼ cup tomato sauce*
2 zucchini, sliced	*1 small French loaf, split*
6 scallions, sliced	*and cut in half*
1 carrot, grated	*8 oz Mozzarella cheese,*
¾ cup sliced mushrooms	*sliced thinly*
⅓ cup whole kernel corn	*salt and pepper to taste*
⅓ cup golden raisins	*marjoram sprigs to garnish*
1 teaspoon chopped	
marjoram	

Serves 4
Preparation time:
5 minutes
Cooking time:
6–7 minutes
Freezing:
Not recommended

1. Heat the oil in a pan, add the zucchini, scallions, carrot, mushrooms, corn, golden raisins, marjoram, and salt and pepper and saute for about 3 minutes.
2. Spread the tomato sauce on the French bread, then cover with the vegetable mixture. Arrange the cheese slices evenly on top.
3. Broil for 3–4 minutes, until bubbling.
4. Garnish with marjoram and serve with a mixed salad.

CHICKEN GOUJONS

Goujons or gudgeons were originally small fish-like whitebait, cooked in egg and breadcrumbs. Here I have used chicken, served with a creamy tarragon sauce.

4 boneless, skinned
  chicken breasts, cut into
  strips
all-purpose flour for
  coating
3 eggs, beaten
4 cups fresh breadcrumbs
1 tablespoon sunflower oil

FOR THE SAUCE:
¹/₄ cup chopped tarragon
¹/₂ cup crème fraîche or
  Greek strained yogurt
salt and pepper to taste
TO GARNISH:
shredded lettuce
lemon wedges

1. Dip the chicken strips in flour to coat, then into the beaten egg and finally coat in the breadcrumbs.
2. Heat the oil in a pan, add the chicken and fry for 5–8 minutes, until golden.
3. Meanwhile, mix all the sauce ingredients together.
4. Serve the goujons on a bed of lettuce, garnished with lemon wedges, and accompanied by the sauce.

Serves 4
Preparation time:
10 minutes
Cooking time:
5–8 minutes
Freezing:
Recommended;
freeze goujons and
sauce separately

HAM AND CELERY ROLLS

This is a traditional English supper dish. Although it is usually made with a Mornay Sauce, I have used a yogurt-based sauce to speed up the process.

4 celery hearts	*1 egg, beaten*
2 tablespoons prepared	*1 cup grated Gruyère*
mustard	*cheese*
4 slices ham	*½ cup fresh breadcrumbs*
1 cup Greek strained	*pepper to taste*
yogurt	*celery leaves to garnish*

Serves 4
Preparation time:
7 minutes
Cooking time:
20 minutes
Freezing:
Not recommended

1. Cook the celery hearts in boiling salted water for 10 minutes; drain.
2. Spread some mustard on each slice of ham and wrap around each celery heart, with the mustard side nearest to the celery. Place in a gratin dish.
3. Mix the remaining mustard with the yogurt, then add the egg, three-quarters of the cheese, and pepper. Pour over the celery hearts.
4. Sprinkle with the breadcrumbs and remaining cheese.
5. Broil for 10 minutes, until golden brown and bubbling.
6. Garnish with celery leaves and serve with bread.

VARIATION
Replace the celery with 4 heads of Belgium endive, cooking them for only 5 minutes before draining.

FUNNY FACES

Young children tend to like food in the shape of faces, trains, cars, etc. They also adore baked beans which, when put with whole wheat toast and given a sprinkling of cheese, make a well-balanced meal. For older children with larger appetites, serve 2 'faces' each.

3 bacon strips, chopped	*2 large whole wheat buns,*
¾ cup sliced mushrooms	*split in half, toasted and*
2 tomatoes, sliced	*buttered*
8 oz can baked beans	*6 oz Cheddar cheese, sliced*
	4 parsley sprigs

1. Gently fry the bacon, add the mushrooms and cook until soft. Drain off any excess fat and set aside 8 mushroom slices.

2. Set aside 2 small tomato slices. Chop the rest, add to the pan with the baked beans and heat through gently.
3. Divide the mixture between the buns and top with the cheese slices.
4. Broil for about 3 minutes, until the cheese is bubbling and melted.
5. Place 2 mushroom slices on each bun half for 'eyes'.
6. Discard the seeds from the reserved tomato slices and cut 4 strips from the flesh for 'mouths'; press in position. Use the parsley sprigs to represent 'noses'. Serve immediately.

Serves 4
Preparation time:
15 minutes
Cooking time:
About 3 minutes
Freezing:
Not recommended

CLUB SANDWICHES

There are endless variations on the traditional club sandwich. Be adventurous and assemble your own combination of favorite ingredients.

8 bacon strips	*12 slices light rye bread,*
1 1/2 cups diced cooked	*toasted and buttered*
chicken	*2 tomatoes, sliced thinly*
1/2 cup mayonnaise	*1/4 cucumber, sliced thinly*
2 Boston lettuce	*1 bunch watercress*
	salt and pepper to taste

Serves 4
Preparation time:
10 minutes
Cooking time:
2 minutes
Freezing:
Not recommended

1. Broil the bacon for 2 minutes, until crisp.
2. Meanwhile, mix the chicken with the mayonnaise, and salt and pepper.
3. Divide the lettuce between 4 of the bread slices and cover with the tomato and cucumber. Top with the bacon.
4. Put another bread slice on top of each. Divide the watercress between the bread and cover with the chicken mixture.
5. Sandwich with the remaining bread and cut in half.

VARIATION
Replace the chicken with sliced roast beef and spread with horseradish sauce; omit the mayonnaise.

FISH CHOWDER

Chowder is a traditional fish soup that is almost a stew. It is made with white fish, shrimp or crab, and a selection of vegetables which usually includes potato.

2 tablespoons sweet butter	*14 oz can chopped*
3 bacon strips, chopped	*tomatoes with herbs*
1 onion, sliced	*1 bay leaf*
2 potatoes, cubed	*7 oz can crab meat*
1 lb cod fillet, skinned and	*(optional)*
cubed	*1/4 cup medium-size*
2 celery sticks, sliced	*shrimp*
2 cups fish stock	*salt and pepper to taste*
	1 tablespoon chopped
	parsley to garnish

1. Melt the butter in a pan, add the bacon and onion and saute for 3 minutes, until soft.

2. Add the potato, cod and celery. Stir until coated in the butter, then add the stock, tomatoes, bay leaf, and salt and pepper. Bring to the boil, cover and simmer gently for 15 minutes.

3. Stir in the crab and shrimp and simmer for 5 minutes until the potato is cooked and the fish is soft, but holding its shape.

4. Transfer to warmed individual bowls and garnish with the parsley. Serve immediately, with crusty rolls.

Serves 4
Preparation time:
10 minutes
Cooking time:
About 25 minutes
Freezing:
Not recommended

TOMATOES WITH GOAT'S CHEESE

Any one of the many types of goat's cheese available can be used for this recipe, but I like to use those called 'Ciganol' —small cheeses preserved in olive oil and herbs.

4 Marmande or Beef tomatoes
4 Ciganol goat's cheeses
1 oakleaf lettuce

2 tablespoons French dressing
½ cup chopped walnuts
basil sprigs to garnish

Serves 4
Preparation time:
5 minutes
Cooking time:
3–5 minutes
Freezing:
Not recommended

1. Make 4 equal cuts through each tomato almost to the base. Cut each goat's cheese into 4 slices and place a slice in each tomato cut.
2. Broil for 3–5 minutes, until the cheese has softened.
3. Divide the lettuce between 4 serving plates and pour over the French dressing. Place the tomatoes alongside, sprinkle with the walnuts and garnish with basil. Serve with crusty French bread.

ITALIAN-STYLE EGGPLANT

Salting and draining eggplant cuts down the amount of fat needed for frying. If you have time, layer the eggplant slices in a colander with salt and leave to stand for at least 15 minutes, then rinse and dry.

2 tablespoons sunflower oil
1 eggplant, sliced thickly

3 oz Parma ham
6 oz Mozzarella cheese, sliced

Serves 4
Preparation time:
3 minutes
Cooking time:
4–5 minutes
Freezing:
Not recommended

1. Heat the oil in a pan, add the eggplant and fry gently until soft. Drain on paper towels.
2. Place a slice of ham on each piece of eggplant and top with a slice of cheese.
3. Place on a baking sheet and broil for 2–3 minutes, until the cheese is just beginning to melt.
4. Serve with a salad and crusty French bread.

CABBAGE WITH BULGUR WHEAT

2 tablespoons sunflower oil	1/2 cup roasted cashew nuts
6 scallions, chopped	1/3 cup raisins
1 inch piece fresh root ginger, chopped finely	2 tomatoes, chopped finely
1 cup bulgur wheat	1 tablespoon chopped parsley
2 1/2 cups chicken stock	1 Savoy cabbage, cut into wedges
1 1/2 teaspoons garam masala	salt and pepper to taste
2 teaspoons soy sauce	lime wedges and mint or parsley sprigs to garnish

Serves 4–6
Preparation time:
10 minutes
Cooking time:
25–30 minutes
Freezing:
Not recommended

1. Heat the oil in a pan, add the scallions and ginger and saute until soft.
2. Stir in the bulgur wheat until it is coated in the oil. Add half of the stock and the garam masala. Bring to the boil, then cover and simmer gently for 10 minutes.
3. Add the soy sauce, nuts, raisins, tomato, parsley, remaining stock, and salt and pepper and simmer for 10–15 minutes, until the bulgur wheat is light and separate.
4. Meanwhile, cook the cabbage in a little boiling salted water for 7–10 minutes, until just tender.
5. Place the bulgur wheat mixture in the center of a warmed serving dish and place the cabbage wedges around the edge.
6. Garnish with lime and mint or parsley to serve.

SPICED RED CABBAGE WITH PINE NUTS AND APRICOTS

This could also be served as an accompaniment to Apple-Tossed Veal (page 58).

2 tablespoons sunflower oil	grated rind and juice of 1 orange
3 1/2 cups shredded red cabbage	1 tablespoon raspberry vinegar
1/3 cup pine nuts	2/3 cup apple cider
1/3 cup chopped dried apricots	salt and pepper to taste
1 teaspoon ground cumin	TO GARNISH:
1 teaspoon ground coriander	kumquat slices
	cilantro leaves

1. Heat the oil in a pan and stir in the cabbage until coated in the oil. Add the pine nuts, apricots, spices, and salt and pepper and saute for 6 minutes.
2. Add the orange rind and juice, raspberry vinegar and cider. Bring to the boil, then cover and simmer for 25 minutes.
3. Transfer to warmed serving plates and garnish with kumquats and cilantro. Serve with bread and cheese.

Serves 4–6
Preparation time
5 minutes
Cooking time:
About 30 minutes
Freezing:
Recommended

VARIATION
Serve raw as a salad: Place the cabbage, nuts and apricots in a serving bowl. Add the spices, orange rind, and salt and pepper. Blend the oil, orange juice and vinegar together, pour over the cabbage and toss well. Omit the cider.

CURRIED VEGETABLES

Vegetables in a mild curry sauce are a lovely way of warming up in the cold winter months. Any combination of vegetables may be used—it's a good way of using up leftovers.

2 tablespoons salad oil	*1 eggplant, sliced*
1 teaspoon cardamom pods	*2 carrots, sliced diagonally*
1 teaspoon cumin seeds	*1 cauliflower, broken into florets*
1 teaspoon chili powder	*¼ lb okra, trimmed*
½ teaspoon ground coriander	*8 oz can peeled tomatoes*
1 clove garlic, crushed	*salt and pepper to taste*
1 onion, sliced	*cilantro leaves to garnish*

Serves 4
Preparation time:
10 minutes
Cooking time:
20 minutes
Freezing:
Recommended

1. Heat the oil in a pan, add the spices and fry for a few seconds.
2. Stir in the garlic, onion, eggplant, carrots, cauliflower and okra and cook for 5 minutes.
3. Add the tomatoes with their juice, and salt and pepper. Bring to the boil, cover and simmer for 15 minutes.
4. Garnish with cilantro and serve with rice.

SAVORY FILLED PITTA BREADS

4 pitta breads
1/2 romaine lettuce or
1 Boston lettuce,
shredded
1/4 cucumber, sliced
1 carrot, grated
1/2 yellow pepper, cored,
seeded and diced
8 oz can red kidney beans,
drained

4 scallions, sliced
1/2 cup grated Cheddar
cheese
FOR THE DRESSING:
2 tablespoons sour
cream
1 teaspoon lemon juice
1/2 teaspoon chili powder

1. Slit each pitta and fill with the salad ingredients.
2. Mix the dressing ingredients together and pour into a small serving bowl.
3. Serve the pitta breads with the dressing.

Serves 4
Preparation time:
10 minutes
Freezing:
Not recommended

VARIATION
Instead of preparing your own vegetables, use a bought prepared salad, e.g. beansprout salad, Bok Choy and mâche salad, apple and raisin salad. Serve with the above dressing, or a little mayonnaise.

CARIBBEAN MONKFISH

Fish is always a good ingredient to cook when in a hurry—it's very nutritious, too.

²/₃ cup unsweetened flaked coconut mixed with 1 cup hot milk
1 teaspoon tomato paste
²/₃ cup dry white wine
1 inch piece fresh root ginger, chopped finely
1 tablespoon chopped cilantro leaves
1 clove garlic, crushed

¹/₂ cup finely chopped onion
2 teaspoon lime juice
1¹/₂ lb monkfish, cut into 2 inch cubes
2 teaspoons cornstarch blended with a little water
lime wedges and cilantro leaves to garnish

Serves 4
Preparation time:
10 minutes
Cooking time:
10–15 minutes
Freezing:
Not recommended

1. Strain the coconut mixture. Place the coconut milk, tomato paste and wine in a frying pan and bring to the boil.
2. Add the remaining ingredients, except the cornstarch, and simmer for 5–10 minutes, until the fish is cooked.
3. Transfer the fish to a warmed serving plate with a fish slice and keep warm.
4. Stir the blended cornstarch into the liquid in the pan and bring to the boil, stirring. Cook for 1 minute, stirring constantly. Pour over the fish.
5. Garnish with lime and cilantro to serve.

ITALIAN-STYLE TAGLIATELLE

Mascarpone is an Italian cream cheese. It is delicious served with coppa, a traditional Italian cured meat which is cheaper than prosciutto.

1 lb fresh tagliatelle
2 cups mascarpone
8 oz coppa, cut into pieces

2 tablespoons grated Parmesan cheese
basil sprigs to garnish

Serves 4
Preparation time:
5 minutes
Cooking time:
5 minutes
Freezing:
Not recommended

1. Cook the pasta according to package instructions; drain well.
2. Place the mascarpone in a large pan and heat gently. Stir in the tagliatelle and coppa.
3. Sprinkle with the Parmesan cheese and garnish with basil to serve.

SEAFOOD PASTA

2 tablespoons butter
2 leeks, sliced
1 clove garlic,
   crushed
1 cup Ricotta cheese
1/3 lb shrimp

1/2 avocado, sliced
1 tablespoon chopped
   parsley
4 tomatoes, quartered
1 lb fresh tagliatelle
chervil sprigs to garnish

1. Melt the butter in a pan, add the leeks and garlic and saute for 5 minutes, until soft. Stir in the Ricotta and allow to melt over a low heat.
2. Stir in the shrimp, avocado, parsley and tomatoes and heat gently, while cooking the pasta.
3. Drain the pasta, place on a warmed serving plate and top with the hot seafood sauce. Garnish with chervil and serve immediately.

Serves 4
Preparation time:
10 minutes
Cooking time:
10 minutes
Freezing:
Not recommended

CREAM OF PEA SOUP

This soup can alternatively be served as a dinner party appetizer, with crisp crackers.

¼ cup butter
4 scallions, chopped
heart of 1 lettuce, shredded
4 cups fresh shelled peas
1 teaspoon sugar
1 teaspoon salt

2½ cups water
1 tablespoon chopped mint
2 tablespoons Greek
strained yogurt
pepper to taste

Serves 4
Preparation time:
5–10 minutes
Cooking time:
15 minutes
Freezing:
Recommended at
end of stage 2

1. Melt the butter in a pan, add the scallions, lettuce, peas, sugar, salt and pepper. Cover and cook gently for 5 minutes.
2. Add the water and mint, bring gradually to the boil, then simmer for 7 minutes. Puree in a food processor or blender.
3. Stir in the yogurt and serve with crusty whole wheat rolls and cheese.

CREAM OF MUSHROOM SOUP

This soup may be served with Melba toast as an appetizer.

1 thick slice bread, crusts
removed
15 oz can chicken
consommé
¼ cup butter
¾ lb mushrooms, chopped
roughly
1 mace blade (optional)

1 teaspoon dried mixed
herbs
pinch of grated nutmeg
¾ cup milk
⅔ cup whipping cream
salt and pepper to taste
chervil sprigs to garnish

Serves 4
Preparation time:
10 minutes
Cooking time:
15–20 minutes
Freezing:
Recommended

1. Soak the bread in a little of the consommé.
2. Melt the butter in a pan, add the mushrooms, mace if using, mixed herbs, nutmeg, and salt and pepper. Cover and cook for 5 minutes.
3. Add the moist bread, remaining consommé and the milk, bring to the boil, then simmer for 10–15 minutes, until the mushrooms are tender.
4. Puree in a blender or food processor. Return to the pan, stir in the cream and reheat gently. Pour into warmed individual bowls and garnish with chervil. Serve with whole wheat bread, and cheese if you wish.

CHICKEN AND VEGETABLE STIR-FRY

*2 tablespoons sunflower
  oil*
*3/4 lb chicken breasts, cut
  into 1/2 inch pieces*
*2 carrots, cut into
  matchstick pieces*
*1 yellow pepper, cored,
  seeded and sliced*
4 scallions, sliced
*15 oz can baby corn cobs,
  drained*

1 cup beansprouts
*1 teaspoon finely chopped
  fresh root ginger*
1/3 cup chicken stock or water
2 tablespoons dry sherry
2 teaspoons soy sauce
*1 teaspoon cornstarch,
  blended with 1 teaspoon
  water*
*scallion curls to garnish
  (see below)*

Serves 4–6
Preparation time:
12 minutes
Cooking time:
10 minutes
Freezing:
Not recommended

1. Heat the oil in a large frying pan or wok, add the chicken pieces and stir-fry for 3 minutes over high heat.
2. Add the vegetables and ginger and stir-fry for 3 minutes.
3. Add the stock or water, sherry, soy sauce and blended cornstarch and bring to the boil, stirring constantly.
4. Serve immediately, garnished with scallion curls.

To make scallion curls: Trim the top and remove the white base. Shred the top, leaving 2 inches attached at the base. Place in ice water until the top curls.

CAULIFLOWER AND BROCCOLI CHEESE

Vegetables play an important part in our diet, because of their fiber and mineral content. Served with crusty whole wheat rolls, this dish provides a well balanced meal.

*1 small cauliflower,
  broken into florets*
1/2 lb broccoli
FOR THE CHEESE SAUCE:
1/2 cup cottage cheese
*3/4 cup grated Cheddar
  cheese*

*1/4 cup cream cheese whipped
  with 1 tablespoon
  lemon juice*
*1 teaspoon prepared
  mustard*
pepper to taste

1. Place the cauliflower in a vegetable steamer or in a large saucepan containing a little boiling water, and steam for 5 minutes. Add the broccoli and cook for 5 minutes or until just tender.
2. Meanwhile, place the sauce ingredients in a non-stick saucepan, beat thoroughly with a wooden spoon and heat

gently until the cheeses melt. Keep warm until the vegetables are cooked.

3. Drain the vegetables well, place in a warmed serving dish and pour over the cheese sauce. Serve with crusty whole wheat rolls.

Serves 4
Preparation time:
5 minutes
Cooking time:
10 minutes
Freezing:
Not recommended

VARIATIONS

1. Replace the cottage cheese with ½ cup low fat Ricotta cheese and add 1 clove garlic and 2 tablespoons chopped parsley.

2. Put the vegetables and sauce into a flameproof serving dish. Sprinkle the finished dish with 1 tablespoon dried whole wheat breadcrumbs and ½ teaspoon grated Parmesan cheese and broil for 2–3 minutes, until golden brown.

SMOKED OYSTER SPINACH PARCELS

½ lb spinach
2 tablespoons butter
¾ cup cottage cheese
2 × 4 oz cans smoked
* oysters, drained*
1 cup finely chopped
* mushrooms*

2 tablespoons chopped
* cilantro leaves*
½ teaspoon garam
* masala*
salt and pepper to taste
TO GARNISH:
lemon wedges
cilantro or parsley sprigs

Serves 4
Preparation time:
10 minutes
Cooking time:
5–7 minutes
Freezing:
Not recommended

1. Place the spinach in a colander standing in a bowl and pour over boiling water. Set aside 20 leaves. Chop the rest very finely.
2. Place the chopped spinach in a bowl, add the remaining ingredients and mix well.
3. Place the reserved spinach leaves on a board and divide the filling between them. Roll up, sealing the edges well.
4. Place the parcels in a steamer, or on a heatproof plate over a pan of simmering water. Cover and steam for 5–7 minutes, until warm.
5. Garnish with lemon wedges and cilantro or parsley and serve with crusty bread.

CHICKEN LIVERS WITH ARTICHOKES

Chicken livers are very quick to cook, and delicious combined with sage and artichoke hearts.

2 tablespoons butter
1 tablespoon olive oil
1 cup sliced onions
1 lb chicken livers
1 tablespoon chopped sage

3 tablespoons sherry or dry
* vermouth*
14 oz can artichoke hearts,
* drained and halved*
salt and pepper to taste
sage leaves to garnish

Serves 4–6
Preparation time:
5 minutes
Cooking time:
10 minutes
Freezing:
Not recommended

1. Melt the butter and oil in a large frying pan until foaming. Add the onions and saute until just soft.
2. Add the chicken livers and sage, saute for a few minutes, then add the remaining ingredients and saute for 6 minutes.
3. Garnish with sage and serve immediately with pasta or crusty French bread.

MUSHROOM AND HERB PATÉ

A good paté for vegetarians. You can use flat or open mushrooms. If you have time, chill before serving. This also makes a tasty dinner party appetizer.

½ cup butter
1 lb mushrooms, chopped
roughly
1 tablespoon tomato juice
or paste
1 tablespoon lemon juice

1 tablespoon dried mixed
herbs
1 teaspoon garlic powder
pepper to taste
TO GARNISH:
lemon or lime slices
marjoram sprigs

Serves 4
Preparation time:
15 minutes
Cooking time:
10 minutes
Freezing:
Not recommended

1. Melt the butter in a pan, add the mushrooms, tomato juice or paste, lemon juice and pepper. Cover and cook for 10 minutes, or until soft.
2. Stir in the mixed dried herbs and garlic powder, place in a food processor or blender and work until smooth.
3. Spoon into 4 ramekins and garnish with lemon or lime slices and marjoram. Serve with whole wheat bread or toast and salad.

HERBY PASTA

There are now many types of fresh pasta available. Any would be suitable for this dish, so try a few different ones.

¼ cup butter
⅓ lb mushrooms, sliced
1 cup sliced onions
¼ cup Greek strained
yogurt
1 cup curd cheese or
farmer's cheese
1 teaspoon garlic powder

1 tablespoon dried mixed
herbs
1 lb paglia e fieno (green
and white noodles)
TO GARNISH:
2 tablespoons grated
Parmesan cheese
parsley sprigs

Serves 4
Preparation time:
10 minutes
Cooking time:
10 minutes
Freezing:
Not recommended

1. Melt the butter in a pan, add the mushrooms and onions and saute until soft. Stir in the yogurt, cheese, garlic powder and mixed herbs, and cook over a low heat until the cheese has just melted.
2. Meanwhile, cook the pasta according to package instructions. Drain, then stir into the hot sauce.
3. Sprinkle the pasta with the Parmesan cheese and serve immediately, garnished with parsley.

QUICK MACKEREL PATÉ

This could also be served as an appetizer for a dinner party.

*2 smoked mackerel,
  skinned, boned and
  flaked*
1/3 cup cream cheese
1 tablespoon mayonnaise
*1 teaspoon grated lemon
  rind*
3 tablespoons lemon juice

*1 tablespoon chopped
  parsley*
1/4 teaspoon paprika
pinch of grated nutmeg
salt and pepper to taste
TO GARNISH:
lemon slices
parsley sprigs

1. Place all the ingredients in a blender or food processor and work until smooth.
2. Spoon into 4 ramekins and garnish with lemon slices and parsley. Serve with whole wheat toast.

Serves 4–6
Preparation time:
10 minutes
Freezing:
Recommended

SALADS

OAKLEAF, MÂCHE AND GRAPE SALAD

Serve this attractive salad with Brie and crusty bread.

2 oz bacon, cut into
strips (optional)
1 oakleaf lettuce
½ lb mâche
¼ lb each black and green
grapes, halved and
seeded

FOR THE DRESSING:
1 tablespoon raspberry
vinegar
3 tablespoons sunflower
oil
1 teaspoon lime juice
1 tablespoon snipped
chives
salt and pepper to taste

Serves 4–6
Preparation time:
10 minutes
Cooking time:
3 minutes
Freezing:
Not recommended

1. Gently fry the bacon, if using, until golden brown. Drain on paper towels.
2. Place the bacon in a serving bowl, add the remaining salad ingredients and toss gently.
3. Place the dressing ingredients in a screw-top jar and shake well to blend. Pour over the salad to serve.

MIDDLE-EASTERN TABBOULEH

Tabbouleh is a traditional Middle-Eastern salad made with bulgur wheat—cracked wheat which has been hulled and parboiled to give it a mild nutty flavor.

1 cup bulgur wheat
6 scallions, chopped
2 tablespoons chopped
mint
¼ cup chopped parsley
3 tablespoons olive oil

¼ cup freshly squeezed
lemon juice
salt and pepper to taste
TO SERVE:
1 small romaine lettuce

Serves 4
Preparation time:
10 minutes, plus
soaking time
Freezing:
Not recommended

1. Place the bulgur wheat in a bowl, cover with cold water and leave to soak for 30 minutes. Squeeze out the water with your hands and place in a bowl.
2. Mix in the remaining ingredients.
3. Arrange the lettuce and tabbouleh in individual serving bowls. Use the lettuce leaves to scoop up the salad.

SPINACH SALAD

There is nothing like the taste of fresh spinach in a salad like this. Spinach is also very good for you as it is high in vitamins and minerals.

1 tablespoon sunflower oil
1 lb young spinach leaves
1 teaspoon grated orange rind
2 tablespoons freshly squeezed orange juice

⅓ cup pine nuts
⅓ cup golden raisins
TO GARNISH:
orange slices
croutons (optional)

Serves 4–6
Preparation time:
5 minutes
Cooking time:
2–3 minutes
Freezing:
Not recommended

1. Heat the oil in a deep saucepan, add the spinach and press down well. Cover and cook for 2–3 minutes, until the leaves have just wilted.
2. Stir in the remaining ingredients and transfer to warmed individual serving dishes.
3. Garnish with orange slices, and croutons if you wish. Serve with rye bread and pastrami.

VARIATION
Replace the spinach leaves with sorrel leaves.

CAULIFLOWER AND BEAN SALAD

½ lb cauliflower florets
15 oz can white kidney beans, drained
4 scallions, sliced
1 tablespoon poppy seeds
salt and pepper to taste
dill sprigs to garnish

FOR THE DRESSING:
3 tablespoons sour cream
1 tablespoon mayonnaise
1 small dessert apple, peeled and grated
1 tablespoon chopped parsley

Serves 4–6
Preparation time:
5 minutes
Cooking time:
2 minutes
Freezing:
Not recommended

1. Blanch the cauliflower in boiling salted water for 2 minutes. Drain and place in a serving bowl with the beans and scallions.
2. Mix all the dressing ingredients together; season with salt and pepper. Pour over the salad and toss well.
3. Sprinkle with the poppy seeds, garnish with dill, and serve with crusty bread.

VARIATION
Add a 4 oz can tuna, drained, to the salad.

AVOCADO AND ENDIVE SALAD

Nasturtium flowers are available in supermarkets. When in season, they make a colorful addition to this salad.

1 head endive
1 avocado, sliced
12 cherry tomatoes
1 package nasturtium
  flowers (optional)
FOR THE DRESSING:
1/3 cup olive oil

2 tablespoons wine
  vinegar
1 teaspoon French
  mustard
1 clove garlic, crushed
1 teaspoon honey
salt and pepper to taste

Serves 4
Preparation time:
5 minutes
Freezing:
Not recommended

1. Arrange the endive leaves, avocado slices and cherry tomatoes on individual serving plates, then sprinkle with the nasturtiums, if using.
2. Mix the dressing ingredients together and pour over the salad. Serve immediately, with a selection of salami and bread.

MEXICAN SALAD

Avocados, peppers and beans are plentiful in Mexico. By combining them, a lovely colorful salad can be made.

8 oz can pineapple pieces
  in natural juice
1 avocado, sliced
1 each yellow and green
  pepper, cored, seeded
  and sliced
2 tomatoes, sliced
1 onion, sliced
8 oz can red kidney beans,
  drained

FOR THE DRESSING:
1 tablespoon lime juice
2 tablespoons sesame oil
1 tablespoon chopped
  cilantro leaves
TO GARNISH:
1 tablespoon desiccated
  coconut, toasted

Serves 2–4
Preparation time:
10 minutes
Freezing:
Not recommended

1. Drain the pineapple, reserving the juice. Mix the pieces with the vegetables and kidney beans and divide between individual serving plates.
2. Make the dressing by mixing the reserved pineapple juice with the remaining ingredients.
3. Pour over the salad and sprinkle with the coconut. Serve with a green salad and tortilla chips.

VARIATION
Replace the coconut with toasted sesame seeds.

BEET SALAD

Beet is such a colorful vegetable and, when used in its raw
state, has a touch of sweetness about it.

4 smoked mackerel fillets,
  flaked into chunks
3/4 lb raw young beet,
  peeled and grated
1 dessert apple, peeled and
  diced

FOR THE DRESSING:
2/3 cup sour cream
2 teaspoons creamed
  horseradish
1 teaspoon chopped dill
salt and pepper to taste

1. Toss the mackerel with the beet and apple, and divide
between individual serving dishes.
2. Mix the dressing ingredients together.
3. Serve the salad with the dressing, and brown bread.

Serves 4
Preparation time:
10 minutes
Freezing:
Not recommended

SMOKED TROUT SALAD

*¾ lb smoked trout fillet,
    skinned
1 ruby red grapefruit,
    peeled and segmented
¼ cucumber, diced
FOR THE DRESSING:
3 tablespoons Greek
    strained yogurt*

*1 tablespoon creamed
    horseradish
1 teaspoon fresh lime juice
1 tablespoon chopped dill
TO GARNISH:
cucumber slices
few endive leaves
dill sprigs*

Serves 4
Preparation time:
10 minutes
Freezing:
Not recommended

1. Flake the trout into bite-size pieces and place in a bowl. Stir in the grapefruit and cucumber.
2. Mix the dressing ingredients together and add to the bowl, tossing carefully.
3. Divide the salad between individual serving plates and garnish with cucumber, endive and dill. Serve with whole wheat bread.

VARIATION
Replace the fresh grapefruit with an 8 oz can grapefruit segments in natural juice, drained.

SUMMER SALAD

You can add anything you like to this salad; e.g. hard-boiled eggs, anchovies, olives, cooked green beans.

*2 Boston or ½ Iceberg
    lettuce
2 ripe tomatoes, quartered
7 oz can tuna, drained
¼ cucumber, sliced
1 red pepper, cored, seeded
    and chopped
2 thin-skinned potatoes,
    boiled and diced*

*FOR THE DRESSING:
⅓ cup olive oil
2 tablespoons wine
    vinegar
2 teaspoons coarse-grain
    mustard
1 tablespoon chopped
    parsley
salt and pepper to taste*

Serves 4
Preparation time:
10 minutes
Freezing:
Not recommended

1. Separate the Boston lettuce into leaves, or cut the Iceberg into chunks. Place in a serving bowl with the remaining salad ingredients.
2. Place the dressing ingredients in a screw-top jar and shake well. Pour over the salad, toss and serve immediately, with French bread.

MIXED BEAN, TUNA AND CORN SALAD

A truly instant meal—perfect for a hot summer's day.

*15 oz jar mixed bean
    salad, drained
7 oz can tuna, drained
7 oz can whole kernel
    corn, drained
2 tablespoons chopped
    parsley*

*1 tablespoon snipped
    chives
2 tablespoons mayonnaise
2 tablespoons sour cream
TO GARNISH:
lettuce leaves
tomato wedges*

Serves 4–6
Preparation time:
5 minutes
Freezing:
Not recommended

1. Place all the ingredients in a bowl and mix well.
2. Divide between individual serving plates and garnish with lettuce and tomato. Serve with warmed whole wheat pitta bread.

SMOKED CHICKEN SALAD

Smoking gives the chicken a moist texture, a delicious flavor, and a longer shelf life.

*¼ lb snow peas
2 smoked chicken breasts,
    shredded
1 each yellow and red
    pepper, cored, seeded
    and sliced
¼ cup pine nuts
2 pieces preserved stem
    ginger, chopped finely
    (optional)
FOR THE DRESSING:
¼ cup olive oil*

*2 tablespoons freshly
    squeezed lime juice
1 tablespoon chopped
    cilantro leaves
1 tablespoon snipped
    chives
salt and pepper to taste
TO GARNISH:
few salad leaves
1 kiwi fruit, sliced*

Serves 4
Preparation time:
10 minutes
Freezing:
Not recommended

1. Blanch the snow peas in boiling salted water for 1 minute. Drain under cold running water.
2. Place in a salad bowl with the remaining salad ingredients.
3. Mix the dressing ingredients together, pour over the salad and toss well.
4. Divide the salad between individual serving plates and garnish with the salad leaves and kiwi fruit. Serve with whole grain bread.

AVOCADO WITH HERB DRESSING

Avocados form the basis of many quick, popular appetizers.

1 avocado, sliced
FOR THE DRESSING:
1/3 cup cream cheese whipped
with 1 tablespoon
lemon juice
2 tablespoons mixed
chopped herbs, e.g. mint,
parsley, chives, chervil

1 clove garlic, crushed
salt and pepper to taste
TO GARNISH:
endive leaves
lime wedges
mint sprigs

Serves 2
Preparation time:
5 minutes
Freezing:
Not recommended

1. Arrange the avocado slices on individual serving plates.
2. Mix the dressing ingredients together and spoon over the avocado.
3. Garnish with endive, lime and mint and serve immediately.

SMOKED SALMON FINGERS

Use Parma ham instead of smoked salmon for this attractive appetizer, if you wish. This could also be served as a lunch or supper dish—when you feel like spoiling your family or friends! Accompany with rye bread or bagels.

1/2 cup curd cheese or
farmer's cheese
1 tablespoon chopped
parsley
1 teaspoon lemon juice
8 thin slices smoked
salmon

pepper to taste
TO GARNISH:
orange wedge
dill sprig
lettuce leaves

Serves 4
Preparation time:
5 minutes
Freezing:
Not recommended

1. Mix the cheese, parsley, lemon juice and pepper together to form a smooth paste.
2. Divide the mixture between the smoked salmon slices, then roll up.
3. Arrange on a serving plate and garnish with orange, dill and lettuce. Serve with thinly sliced whole wheat bread.

ZUCCHINI FANS

This is a very attractive salad to serve as an appetizer or accompaniment. It is eaten warm and is delicious!

1 lb small zucchini
¼ lb cherry tomatoes,
sliced
2 scallions, chopped
basil sprigs to garnish

FOR THE DRESSING:
6 tablespoons olive oil
2 tablespoons lemon juice
1 tablespoon each chopped
chives, basil and chervil
salt and pepper to taste

Serves 4
Preparation time:
5 minutes
Cooking time:
5–7 minutes
Freezing:
Not recommended

1. Cook the zucchini whole in boiling salted water for 5–7 minutes, until just soft. Drain well, then cut in half lengthways.
2. Place the halves cut side down and slice lengthways, leaving about ½ inch at the end to keep them together.
3. Place the zucchini on individual serving plates and press gently to open out like fans. Arrange the tomatoes and scallions at the top.
4. Mix the dressing ingredients together and pour over the salad. Garnish with basil and serve while the zucchini are still warm.

MUSSEL SALAD

3 × 7 oz cans mussels in
vinegar, drained
¾ cup crème fraîche, or
¾ cup cream cheese
whipped with 3 table-
spoons lemon juice
2 tablespoons raspberry
vinegar

2 tablespoons chopped
chervil
1 tablespoon chopped
tarragon
salt and pepper to taste
few salad leaves to serve

Serves 4
Preparation time:
5 minutes
Freezing:
Not recommended

1. Place the mussels in a bowl and stir in the remaining ingredients.
2. Arrange the salad leaves on individual serving plates with the mussel salad. If there is time, chill for up to 2 hours. Serve with dark rye bread.

VARIATION
Replace the raspberry vinegar with tarragon vinegar.

CREAM OF WATERCRESS SOUP

3 tablespoons butter
2 bunches watercress,
  chopped roughly
½ cup chopped onions
2 tablespoons chopped
  parsley

1 tablespoon all-purpose
  flour
15 oz can chicken
  consommé
⅔ cup Greek strained
  yogurt

1. Melt the butter in a pan, add the watercress, onions and parsley, cover and cook gently for 5 minutes, to allow the juices to run.
2. Stir in the flour and cook for 1 minute, without browning.
3. Gradually stir in the consommé, bring to the boil, then simmer for 3 minutes.
4. Puree in a blender or food processor.
5. Stir in two thirds of the yogurt and reheat gently. Swirl the remaining yogurt on each portion to serve.

Serves 4
Preparation time:
5 minutes
Cooking time:
9 minutes
Freezing:
Recommended, at
end of stage 4

TOMATO AND ORANGE SOUP

The combination of oranges and tomato is mouth-watering. Make this soup in the summer when tomatoes are plentiful, and serve chilled if you prefer.

8 medium-size ripe
   tomatoes, chopped
1/2 cup chopped onions
1 carrot, grated
2 tablespoons chopped
   basil
2 tablespoons grated
   orange rind
1/4 cup freshly squeezed
   orange juice

1 teaspoon superfine sugar
3 3/4 cups chicken stock
1 cup Greek strained
   yogurt
1/4 teaspoon grated
   nutmeg
salt and pepper to taste
1 tablespoon snipped
   chives to garnish

Serves 4–6
Preparation time:
10 minutes
Cooking time:
15–20 minutes
Freezing:
Recommended, at
end of stage 2

1. Place all the ingredients, except the yogurt and nutmeg, in a saucepan. Bring to the boil, then simmer for 15–20 minutes, until the tomatoes are tender.
2. Puree in a food processor or blender, then sieve.
3. Return to the pan, stir in the yogurt and nutmeg and heat gently; do not boil.
4. Pour into individual soup dishes and sprinkle with the chives. Serve with crackers.

MUSSEL AND SAFFRON SOUP

This is a traditional French recipe, variations of which can be found in the tiny fishing villages on the south-west coast of France. The saffron is infused in the fish stock to give a lovely yellow color, which blends attractively with the orange color of the mussels.

2¹/₂ cups fish stock
2 tablespoons dry sherry
¹/₄ teaspoon garlic powder
¹/₂ teaspoon mild curry
* powder*
1 package saffron strands

2 × 8 oz cans mussels in
* brine, drained*
2 egg yolks
²/₃ cup heavy cream
salt and pepper to taste
chopped parsley to garnish

1. Bring the fish stock to just below boiling and stir in the sherry, garlic powder, curry powder, saffron, and salt and pepper. Strain, then add the mussels and heat gently for 5 minutes.
2. Mix the egg yolks with the cream, then stir into the soup and heat gently for 3 minutes; do not allow to boil.
3. Pour into individual soup bowls and serve immediately, garnished with parsley.

Serves 4
Preparation time:
5 minutes
Cooking time:
8 minutes
Freezing:
Not recommended

ITALIAN RISOTTO

Italian risotto rice has round medium-size grains, a slightly chewy texture and creamy color. It is the traditional rice for risottos, but if you prefer you can use long-grain brown or white rice.

1/4 cup butter
1 tablespoon olive oil
1 small onion, chopped
1 1/2 cups sliced mushrooms
3/4 lb chicken livers, chopped roughly
2 tomatoes, chopped
1 yellow pepper, cored, seeded and chopped
3/4 cup Italian risotto rice
few saffron threads

1 tablespoon chopped sage
2 1/2 cups hot chicken stock
2/3 cup white wine
2 tablespoons dry vermouth
1 tablespoon grated Parmesan cheese
2 tablespoons chopped parsley (optional)
salt and pepper to taste
parsley sprigs to garnish

Serves 4
Preparation time:
20 minutes
Cooking time:
25–30 minutes
Freezing:
Not recommended

1. Heat half of the butter and the oil in a large heavy-based pan, add the onion, mushrooms and chicken livers and saute until the onion is soft and the chicken livers sealed and brown. Add the tomatoes and yellow pepper.
2. Stir in the rice and saute until transparent, stirring constantly.
3. Add the saffron threads and sage to the hot chicken stock. Add 2/3 cup of the stock to the rice, bring to the boil, stirring constantly, then simmer for about 10 minutes until it has nearly all been absorbed. Add the remaining stock, wine and vermouth and simmer for 25–30 minutes until all the liquid has been absorbed and the rice is tender.
4. Stir in the remaining butter, the Parmesan cheese, parsley if using, and salt and pepper.
5. Transfer to a warmed serving dish and garnish with parsley.

VEAL WITH LEMON AND LIME

This is a very quick and simple but filling dinner party dish. For best results, the veal escalopes should be no more than ¼ inch thick.

4 veal escalopes, each
*   about ⅓ lb*
seasoned flour for coating
2 eggs, beaten
2 cups fresh breadcrumbs
1 tablespoon olive oil

¼ cup sweet butter
juice of 1 lemon
juice of 1 lime
lime or lemon slices to
*   garnish*

1. Dip each escalope into seasoned flour, then into beaten egg and finally into the breadcrumbs to coat evenly.
2. Heat the oil and butter in a frying pan until foaming, add 2 veal escalopes and half of the lemon and lime juice and fry for 3–4 minutes on each side. Keep warm while cooking the remaining escalopes.
3. Garnish with lime or lemon slices and serve with green beans or zucchini and thin-skinned potatoes.

Serves 4
Preparation time:
5 minutes
Cooking time:
12–16 minutes
Freezing:
Not recommended

ROULADES OF SALMON, SPINACH AND LEMON SOLE

These make an attractive light main course; alternatively they can be served as an appetizer for a special dinner.

1/4 lb smoked salmon
2 lemon sole, skinned and
   filleted
1/2 lb spinach leaves,
   central ribs removed
2/3 cup dry white wine
1 bay leaf
1 parsley sprig
1 tarragon sprig
salt and pepper to taste

FOR THE SPINACH SAUCE:
2 tablespoons butter
1/4 cup chopped onion
1/4 teaspoon garlic powder
1 bay leaf
1 1/4 cups vegetable stock
2/3 cup dry white wine
3/4 cup crème fraîche, or
   cream cheese whipped
   with 3 tablespoons
   lemon juice

Serves 4
Preparation time:
15 minutes
Cooking time:
8–10 minutes
Freezing:
Not recommended

1. Cut the salmon into strips the approximate length and width of the lemon sole.
2. Place a spinach leaf on a sole fillet, top with a piece of smoked salmon, then cover with another spinach leaf. Roll up tightly and secure with a wooden cocktail stick.
3. Place the rolls in a pan and add the wine, herbs, and salt and pepper. Cover and cook gently for 8–10 minutes, until the fish is cooked. Remove from the pan with a slotted spoon and keep warm.
4. Meanwhile, make the spinach sauce. Melt the butter in a pan, add the onion, garlic powder and remaining spinach, cover and cook gently for about 5 minutes, until the juices run.
5. Add the bay leaf, stock and wine, bring to the boil and boil until reduced by about half. Discard the bay leaf. Puree the mixture in a food processor or blender.
6. Stir in the crème fraîche or cream cheese mixture, return to the saucepan and simmer gently for 2 minutes.
7. Spoon the spinach sauce onto a warmed serving plate and arrange the fish roulades on top. Serve immediately.

VARIATION
Use fresh salmon instead of smoked salmon and turbot fillets instead of lemon sole.

STIR-FRIED GINGERED BEEF

2 teaspoons soy sauce
1 tablespoon sherry
1 teaspoon sesame oil
1 teaspoon cornstarch
1 inch piece fresh root
  ginger, grated
grated rind of 1 orange
  and 1 tablespoon juice

¾–1 lb beef fillet,
  shredded into strips ½
  inch wide
1 tablespoon sunflower oil
¼ lb snow peas
4 oz can water chestnuts,
  drained and sliced
orange segments to
  garnish

1. Place the soy sauce, sherry, sesame oil, cornstarch, ginger, orange rind and juice in a bowl. Stir in the beef and leave to marinate for at least 15 minutes. Remove the beef with a slotted spoon; reserve the marinade.
2. Heat the sunflower oil in a large frying pan or wok, add the beef and stir-fry for 3–5 minutes, until browned.
3. Stir in the marinade, snow peas and water chestnuts and cook for 5 minutes.
4. Serve immediately, garnished with orange and accompanied by rice or noodles.

Serves 4
Preparation time:
5 minutes, plus marinating
Cooking time:
8–10 minutes
Freezing:
Not recommended

PHEASANT WITH PLUM SAUCE

Pheasant breast joints as well as whole pheasants are now available in many supermarkets. If you buy the breast joint, cut down the breast bone with kitchen scissors or poultry scissors to divide the joint.

4 strips bacon
2 pheasant breasts
1/4 cup butter
1 tablespoon olive oil
2 celery sticks, chopped
1 teaspoon lemon juice
salt and pepper to taste
salad leaves to garnish

FOR THE PLUM SAUCE:
3/4 cup chicken stock or
consommé
2 tablespoons tomato juice
3 tablespoons plum
conserve
2 tablespoons white wine
1 teaspoon juniper berries,
crushed

Serves 2
Preparation time:
5 minutes
Cooking time:
25 minutes
Freezing:
Not recommended

1. Wrap 2 bacon strips around each pheasant breast.
2. Heat the butter and oil in a heavy-based pan until foaming. Add the pheasant breasts and cook quickly over high heat to seal and brown well all over. Add the celery, lemon juice, and salt and pepper. Cover and cook for 25 minutes, turning occasionally.
3. Ten minutes before the cooking time is up, prepare the sauce. Place all the ingredients in a saucepan and heat gently until the conserve has melted, then simmer gently for 7 minutes.
4. Remove the pheasant and drain on paper towels. Serve immediately, accompanied by the sauce, and garnished with the salad leaves.

VARIATION
Replace the pheasant with duck breasts: prick skins first, do not use bacon, and cook for only 7–10 minutes.

LAMB WITH CRANBERRY SAUCE

8 lamb cutlets
olive oil for brushing
few thyme sprigs
salt and pepper to taste
few watercress sprigs to
garnish
FOR THE CRANBERRY
SAUCE:
1/4 cup cranberry sauce

1 tablespoon port or
full-bodied red wine
1 teaspoon lemon juice
1 cup cranberries
1 teaspoon grated orange
rind
1 tablespoon freshly
squeezed orange juice

1. Place the lamb cutlets in a broiling pan, brush with olive oil, season liberally with salt and pepper and sprinkle with the thyme sprigs.
2. Broil for 3–5 minutes on each side, according to taste.
3. Meanwhile, place the sauce ingredients in a saucepan and heat gently.
4. Pour a pool of sauce onto 4 warmed serving plates and place 2 cutlets on each. Garnish with watercress and serve with green vegetables or a green salad.

Serves 4
Preparation time:
5 minutes
Cooking time:
6–10 minutes
Freezing:
Not recommended

VARIATION
Replace the lamb cutlets with lamb fillet: slice and fry with the thyme in 2 tablespoons butter. Serve with the cranberry sauce as above.

BROILED SCALLOPS

Scallops can be bought fresh or frozen. They are delicious served with a tomato coulis as a light main course, or you could halve the ingredients and serve as an appetizer.

16 strips bacon	*1 tablespoon olive oil*
16 scallops	*1 teaspoon superfine sugar*
FOR THE TOMATO	*1 tablespoon freshly*
COULIS:	*squeezed orange juice*
4 medium-size tomatoes	*1/2 teaspoon paprika*
2 small onions	*salt and pepper to taste*

Serves 4
Preparation time:
5 minutes
Cooking time:
8–10 minutes
Freezing:
Not recommended

1. Stretch the bacon strips, using the back of a knife, and wrap around the scallops. Thread onto 4 skewers and broil for 8–10 minutes, turning several times.
2. Meanwhile, make the sauce. Place all the ingredients in a food processor or blender and work until smooth. Place in a saucepan, bring to the boil, then simmer for 8 minutes. Rub through a fine sieve to form a smoother sauce, if you wish.
3. Pour some sauce on each warmed serving plate and place a skewer of broiled scallops on top. Serve with fresh pasta and a crunchy salad.

VARIATION
Replace the scallops with large shrimp, shelled.

HONEY-GLAZED GAME HENS

These glazed and broiled little birds would be good barbecued, too. Depending on the appetite of your guests and the size of the game hens, this recipe will serve 2 or 4.

2 Rock Cornish game hens	*2 tablespoons freshly*
FOR THE BASTING SAUCE:	*squeezed orange juice*
1/4 cup honey	*1 green chili, seeded and*
1 tablespoon wine vinegar	*chopped finely*
1 teaspoon soy sauce	*salt and pepper to taste*
1 tablespoon sunflower oil	*TO SERVE:*
1 inch piece fresh root	*15 oz can baby corn cobs*
ginger, peeled and	*1 tablespoon sunflower oil*
chopped finely	*1 cup beansprouts*

1. Split the game hens in half along the backbone and breastbone, using kitchen scissors. With a sharp knife slit the skin once.
2. Mix the basting ingredients together, then brush over the pieces of game hen.
3. Line a broiling pan with foil. Place the game hens in the pan and broil for 15–20 minutes, basting frequently and turning occasionally.
4. Meanwhile, heat the baby corn cobs in a saucepan as directed on the can.
5. Heat the oil and stir-fry the beansprouts for a few seconds.
6. To serve, arrange the game hens, corn and beansprouts on warmed serving plates.

Serves 2 or 4
Preparation time:
5 minutes
Cooking time:
15–20 minutes
Freezing:
Not recommended

VARIATION
Replace the game hens with 4 or 8 chicken drumsticks.

APPLE-TOSSED VEAL

The addition of Calvados, an apple brandy, makes all the difference to this recipe. If you wish, heat it first, ignite, then add to the veal while still flaming.

4 veal escalopes, each weighing about ¼ lb and ¼ inch thick
2 tablespoons all-purpose flour
¼ cup butter
1 tablespoon olive oil
1 dessert apple, peeled, cored and sliced thinly

1 tablespoon Dijon mustard
1 tablespoon chopped sage
2 tablespoons Calvados
¼ cup crème fraîche, or cream cheese whipped with 1 tablespoon lemon juice
salt and pepper to taste
sage leaves to garnish

Serves 4
Preparation time:
5 minutes
Cooking time:
10 minutes
Freezing:
Not recommended

1. Dust the veal with the flour. Heat the butter and oil in a large pan until foaming, add the veal and cook quickly to brown both sides.
2. Add the apple, mustard, sage, Calvados, and salt and pepper. Saute for 3–5 minutes, until the veal is cooked. Transfer the veal to a warmed serving dish.
3. Stir the crème fraîche or cream cheese mixture into the pan. Spoon the sauce over the veal and garnish with sage. Serve with thin-skinned potatoes and a green vegetable or Spiced Red Cabbage with Pine Nuts and Apricots (page 20).

VENISON WITH SPICED CHERRY SAUCE

For this recipe you need to use meat from a young deer as it is delicate in flavor and does not need marinating.

12 juniper berries, crushed
4 venison fillets, each about ⅓ lb and 1 inch thick
¼ cup butter
1 tablespoon olive oil
salt and pepper to taste
watercress sprigs to garnish
FOR THE CHERRY SAUCE:
12 oz can sour cherries in syrup

¼ teaspoon ground cinnamon
3 cloves
⅔ cup full-bodied red wine
1 tablespoon lemon juice
2 teaspoons arrowroot, blended with a little water

1. First, make the sauce. Drain and pit the cherries, reserving the syrup. Place the cherries, cinnamon, cloves, wine and lemon juice in a saucepan. Bring to the boil, then simmer gently for 10 minutes.
2. Meanwhile, rub the juniper berries and salt and pepper into the venison steaks.
3. Melt the butter and oil in a pan until foaming, add the venison and fry quickly on both sides to seal, then lower the heat and cook for 8 minutes, turning once. Transfer to a warmed serving dish and keep warm.
4. Stir a little of the cherry sauce into the blended arrowroot, then return to the sauce in the pan. Bring to the boil, stirring until thickened.
5. Garnish the venison with the watercress and serve with the cherry sauce. Serve hot chestnut puree or celeriac puree as an accompaniment.

Serves 4
Preparation time:
5 minutes
Cooking time:
10–15 minutes
Freezing:
Not recommended

VARIATION
Use lamb cutlets instead of venison steaks.

DUCK BREASTS IN ORANGE SAUCE

Duck is a fattier meat than any other poultry; pricking it all over makes it easier for the fat to escape. The flavor is also stronger, so the combination of orange complements the duck very well.

4 duck breast fillets,
  skinned
1 tablespoon honey
3 oranges
1 tablespoon olive oil
1/2 bunch watercress
FOR THE ORANGE SAUCE:
1 tablespoon sugar
1 tablespoon wine vinegar

2 tablespoons brandy
3/4 cup freshly squeezed
  orange juice
1/4 lb kumquats, sliced
  (optional)
2 teaspoons cornstarch,
  blended with 2 table-
  spoons orange juice

Serves 4
Preparation time:
10 minutes
Cooking time:
12 minutes
Freezing:
Recommended

1. Prick the duck all over and brush with the honey. Grate the rind from 1 orange and sprinkle over the duck.
2. Heat the oil in a pan, add the duck and fry for 6 minutes on each side. Keep warm.
3. To make the orange sauce, place the sugar and vinegar in a heavy-based saucepan and heat gently until the sugar has dissolved and it is a golden caramel color.
4. Carefully add the brandy, orange juice and kumquats, if using, and simmer gently for 5 minutes.
5. Add a little of the hot sauce to the blended cornstarch and mix well. Return to the saucepan, bring to the boil, then cook for 2–3 minutes, stirring, until thickened.
6. Segment all the oranges, removing all the pith. Arrange the watercress and orange segments on 4 warmed serving plates.
7. Slice the duck breasts lengthways and arrange on the plates. Pour over a little sauce to serve.

GINGERED SHRIMP

2 tablespoons olive oil
1 lb large shelled shrimp
2 inch piece fresh root
  ginger, chopped
1/4 teaspoon ground
  ginger
1 teaspoon chopped
  cilantro leaves

6 scallions, chopped
1 papaya, halved, seeded
  and chopped
1 teaspoon grated lime
  rind
3 tablespoons lime juice
salt and pepper to taste
salad leaves to garnish

1. Heat the oil in a pan, add the shrimp, chopped fresh and ground ginger, cilantro leaves, scallions, and salt and pepper, and saute for 3 minutes.'
2. Stir in the papaya, lime rind and juice and saute for 2 minutes.
3. Transfer to warmed individual serving plates and garnish with salad leaves.

Serves 4–6
Preparation time:
5 minutes
Cooking time:
5 minutes
Freezing:
Not recommended

VARIATION
If large shrimp are unavailable, replace with 1 lb monkfish, cut into 1 inch cubes.

DESSERTS

CHERRIES IN RED WINE

This is a very simple but pleasant way of serving fruit such as cherries, pears and peaches. I suggest using a Beaujolais or rosé wine, to complement the flavor of the fruit.

1 1/4 cups Beaujolais or
rosé wine
1/3 cup vanilla sugar (see
below)
1 cinnamon stick

3 cloves
1 lb cherries, pitted
mint leaves to decorate
(optional)

Serves 4–6
Preparation time:
10 minutes
Cooking time:
5 minutes
Freezing:
Not recommended

1. Place the wine, sugar, cinnamon stick and cloves in a saucepan and heat gently until the sugar has dissolved.
2. Stir in the cherries, bring to the boil, then simmer for 5 minutes. Remove the cinnamon stick and cloves.
3. Decorate with mint if you wish, and serve warm or cold, with heavy cream or Greek strained yogurt.

NOTE: Vanilla sugar is easily made: place a vanilla pod in a screw-top jar and fill up with superfine sugar. The pod will impart a vanilla flavor to the sugar if left to stand for at least a week.

SUMMER MERINGUE NESTS

2 1/2 cups blueberry ice
cream

6 meringue nests
1 3/4 cups raspberries

Serves 6
Preparation time:
5 minutes
Freezing:
Not recommended

1. Place a large scoop of blueberry ice cream in each meringue nest and place on individual serving plates, with the raspberries.
2. Serve immediately.

VARIATIONS

1. Place an extra ½ cup raspberries, 1 tablespoon powdered sugar and 1 teaspoon lemon juice in a blender or food processor and puree to make a sauce. Sieve to remove seeds. Pour the raspberry sauce over the meringue nests to serve.
2. Replace the blueberry ice cream with strawberry ice cream and the raspberries with strawberries.

FRUIT MELBA

I have used strawberry ice cream for this dessert, but there are several others flavors that would be equally good with the sauce and fruit, e.g. spumoni, peach melba.

*4 nectarines or peaches,
  halved and pitted
2 cups strawberry ice
  cream
FOR THE MELBA SAUCE:
1 cup raspberries*

*¹/₂ cup powdered sugar,
  sifted
1 teaspoon lemon juice
TO DECORATE (optional):
1 tablespoon chopped nuts*

Serves 4
Preparation time:
10 minutes
Freezing:
Recommended for
the melba sauce
only

1. First, prepare the melba sauce. Puree the raspberries in a food processor or blender. Stir in the powdered sugar and lemon juice.
2. Place 2 nectarine or peach halves in each individual serving dish and top each with a scoop of ice cream. Pour over the melba sauce.
3. Decorate with chopped nuts, if you wish.

APPLE SNOW

This is a lovely light creamy dessert that I used to enjoy as a child. You can, of course, make your own custard if you wish, using the egg yolk.

*3 cups sliced cooking
  apples, cooked with
  2 tablespoons sugar
  until soft, or 15 oz can
  stewed apples*

*15 oz can custard
1 egg white
mint sprigs to decorate
ladies' fingers to serve*

Serves 4
Preparation time:
5–15 minutes
Freezing:
Not recommended

1. Puree the stewed apple in a food processor or blender. Mix with the custard.
2. Whisk the egg white until stiff peaks form, then fold into the apple mixture.
3. Pour into serving dishes, garnish with mint and serve with ladies' fingers.

VARIATION
Use stewed gooseberries instead of apples.

PRUNE AND FILBERT WHIP

*15 oz can prunes in fruit
juice*
*½ cup chopped filberts,
roasted*

*1 cup Greek strained
yogurt*
1 tablespoon honey
2 egg whites

1. Pit the prunes and reserve the juice. Place the prunes and 2 tablespoons of the juice in a food processor or blender and work until smooth.
2. Set aside 1 tablespoon of the filberts for decoration. Stir the rest into the prune puree with the yogurt and honey.
3. Whisk the egg whites until soft peaks form, then fold into the prune mixture.
4. Spoon into individual serving dishes and decorate with the reserved filberts.

Serves 4–6
Preparation time:
5 minutes
Freezing:
Not recommended

STRAWBERRY DREAM

This is a lovely light dessert, with a decliate pink color. The addition of rosewater enhances the flavor of the strawberries.

1 lb strawberries
2 tablespoons powdered sugar (optional)
²/₃ cup cream cheese whipped with 3 tablespoons lemon juice

1 tablespoon rosewater
1¹/₄ cups heavy cream, whipped
thin shortbread cookies to serve

Serves 4–6
Preparation time:
5 minutes
Freezing:
Not recommended

1. Mash the strawberries together with the powdered sugar, if using.
2. Stir the cream cheese mixture and rosewater into the cream, then stir into the strawberries.
3. Spoon into individual serving dishes and serve with thin shortbread cookies.

VARIATION
Replace the cream cheese mixture with Greek yogurt.

REDCURRANT TARTS

These delightful little tarts are ideal for *al fresco* summer parties. If fresh redcurrants cannot be found, use canned or frozen ones.

1/2 cup superfine sugar
2/3 cup rosé wine
1 lb redcurrants

2 tablespoons redcurrant jelly
6 individual tart cases

Serves 6
Preparation time:
10 minutes
Freezing:
Not recommended

1. Place the sugar and wine in a saucepan and heat gently until dissolved. Add the redcurrants, cover and cook gently for 3 minutes. Remove with a slotted spoon and set aside.
2. Boil the liquid for a few minutes, until reduced and syrupy. Stir in the redcurrant jelly and heat gently until melted.
3. Divide the redcurrants between the tart cases and brush them with the glaze.
4. Serve with Greek strained yogurt or whipped cream.

VARIATION
Replace the redcurrants with blueberries.

CRUNCHY-TOPPED BANANA SPLIT

An age-old favorite. I've sprinkled the top with crunchy oat cereal and golden raisins, but use chopped nuts if you prefer. The chocolate sauce can be made beforehand and melted gently when required.

*4 bananas, split in half
  lengthways
2 1/2 cups maple and
  walnut ice cream
1/4 cup crunchy oat cereal
2 tablespoons golden
  raisins*

*FOR THE HOT
  CHOCOLATE SAUCE:
8 oz baker's semi-sweet
  chocolate
1/2 cup light brown sugar,
  packed
1 1/4 cups hot water
2 tablespoons butter*

Serves 4
Preparation time:
10 minutes
Freezing:
Not recommended

1. First, make the sauce. Place the chocolate, sugar and water in a heavy-based saucepan and heat gently until the chocolate has melted; boil until it coats the back of the spoon. Cool slightly, then beat in the butter.
2. Arrange the bananas in 4 individual serving dishes with scoops of the ice cream. Pour over the chocolate sauce.
3. Sprinkle with the cereal and golden raisins and serve at once.

VARIATION

Serve with butterscotch sauce instead of chocolate: melt 1/4 cup each butter, light brown sugar and corn syrup in a heavy-based saucepan, then bring to the boil and boil until it reaches soft ball stage—that is, when a little of the mixture is dropped into cold water it forms a soft ball. Cool slightly, then gradually beat in 2/3 cup milk.

LEMON AND LIME CREAMS

*grated rind and juice of 1
  lemon and 1 lime
1/2 cup curd or farmer's
  cheese
2 tablespoons honey*

*2/3 cup whipping cream,
  whipped
3 oz crunchy oat cereal
lime slices to decorate*

Serves 4–6
Preparation time:
7 minutes, plus
chilling
Freezing:
Not recommended

1. Mix the fruit rinds and juice with the cheese and honey. Fold in the cream.
2. Place about 1 tablespoon cereal in each serving dish and place the citrus cream on top. Chill until required.
3. Decorate with lime slices to serve.

WATERMELON, KIWI FRUIT AND BANANA SALAD

1 tablespoon lime juice
2 tablespoons ginger wine
2 inch piece fresh root
ginger, grated
1 tablespoon superfine
sugar (optional)
1 large slice watermelon

2 kiwi fruit, peeled and
sliced
1 banana, sliced
¼ lb green grapes, seeded
mint sprig to decorate
(optional)

1. Place the lime juice, ginger wine, ginger and sugar, if using, in a pan and heat gently. Leave to cool.
2. Remove the seeds and skin from the watermelon and cut into thin slices.
3. Mix all the fruit together and place in a serving dish. Pour over the syrup.
4. Decorate with the mint sprig, if using, to serve.

Serves 4
Preparation time:
10 minutes
Freezing:
Not recommended

GOOSEBERRY TART

The addition of a few redcurrants or raspberries gives the tart an extra dash of color.

*1 lb gooseberries, topped
and tailed
²/₃ cup Moselle wine
2 tablespoons honey
10 inch tart case*

*½ cup redcurrants or
raspberries
3 tablespoons redcurrant
jelly, melted*

Serves 8–10
Preparation time:
5 minutes
Cooking time:
5 minutes
Freezing:
Recommended

1. Place the gooseberries, wine and honey in a pan, cover and cook very gently for 5 minutes, until just tender; drain.
2. Place the gooseberries in the tart case, then drop in the redcurrants or raspberries at random. Pour over the melted redcurrant jelly to glaze.
3. Serve with Devon clotted cream, whipped cream or Greek strained yogurt.

VARIATION
Replace the gooseberries with apples and decorate with blackberries or blueberries.

CHESTNUT PAVLOVAS

A quick, beautiful and very rich dessert. If only un-sweetened chestnut puree can be obtained, stir in ½ cup sifted powdered sugar.

*²/₃ cup heavy cream
9 oz sweetened chestnut
puree*

*2 tablespoons brandy
4 meringue nests
grated chocolate to serve*

Serves 4
Preparation time:
5 minutes
Freezing:
Recommended for
filling only

1. Whip the cream until just beginning to form soft peaks. Gradually fold into the chestnut puree, then stir in the brandy.
2. Pipe or spoon the mixture into the meringue nests.
3. Sprinkle the meringue with grated chocolate and serve with extra cream.

VARIATION
Melt 3 oz baker's semi-sweet chocolate, cool slightly, then stir into the chestnut puree.

KNICKERBOCKER GLORY

A favorite British dessert. Use any combination of fruit and ice cream you fancy, such as Cherry Kirsch and Passion Fruit ice creams with sliced kiwi fruit. Serve in tall glasses.

7 oz can apricot halves in
fruit juice
1 cup Honey and Ginger
ice cream
1 cup orange sorbet
1 cup raspberries

TO DECORATE (optional):
²⁄₃ cup whipping cream,
whipped
1 tablespoon chopped
roasted filberts

Serves 6
Preparation time:
7–10 minutes
Freezing:
Not recommended

1. Drain the apricots, reserving the juice. Puree the apricots and ⅓ cup of the juice in a food processor or blender.
2. Fill 6 tall chilled glasses with alternate layers of ice cream, sorbet and raspberries. Pour some apricot sauce into each glass.
3. Decorate with a spoonful of whipped cream and sprinkle with filberts if you wish.

VARIATION
Replace the apricots with 7 oz can raspberries in fruit juice.

TROPICAL FRUIT SALAD

This is a very colorful fruit salad. Depending on time and availability, fresh or canned fruit can be used.

1 mango, sliced, or 15 oz
can mango slices in
syrup, drained
8 oz can pineapple pieces
in natural juice,
drained or ½ fresh
pineapple, peeled
and sliced

1 papaya, sliced
1 tablespoon lime juice
1 tablespoon rum
(optional)
1 tablespoon desiccated
coconut, toasted
(optional)
lime wedges to serve

Serves 4–6
Preparation time:
5–15 minutes
Freezing:
Not recommended

1. Arrange the fruit on individual serving plates.
2. Pour over the lime juice, and rum if using. Sprinkle with coconut, if you wish, and serve with lime wedges.

OLD-FASHIONED TRIFLE

A luscious dessert suitable for any occasion. Replace the canned fruit with fresh fruit, if you prefer.

4 oz pound cake, cubed
⅓ cup sherry
11 oz can mandarins in natural juice, drained
8 oz can pineapple pieces in natural juice, drained

7 oz can strawberries in fruit juice, drained
⅔ cup heavy cream, whipped
15 oz can custard
TO DECORATE:
2–3 glacé cherries, halved
few pieces angelica

1. Place the pound cake in individual dishes and sprinkle with the sherry. Place the mandarins, pineapple and strawberries on top.
2. Set aside 2–3 tablespoons of the cream. Stir the remainder into the custard and spoon over the fruit.
3. Decorate with the remaining cream, the glacé cherries and angelica.

Serves 4–6
Preparation time: 5 minutes
Freezing: Not recommended

ZABAGLIONE

This is a delicious dinner party dessert, but it does have to be made and served immediately. The Marsala gives it its traditional Italian flavor.

6 egg yolks, beaten
½ cup superfine sugar
5–6 tablespoons Marsala

amaretti biscuits or
macaroons to serve
(optional)

Serves 4–6
Preparation time:
15 minutes
Freezing:
Not recommended

1. Place all the ingredients in a large bowl over a pan of hot water, or in a double boiler. Beat for about 10 minutes until the mixture becomes thick and creamy.
2. Pour into serving glasses and serve immediately, with amaretti biscuits or macaroons, if you wish.

SUMMER FRUIT SALAD

1 cantaloup or charentais
melon
¼ lb redcurrants
2 apricots, sliced
1 peach, sliced
2 tablespoons freshly
squeezed orange juice

1 teaspoon grated orange
rind
1 tablespoon superfine
sugar (optional)
1 tablespoon eau-de-vie de
framboise or kirsch
(optional)

Serves 4–6
Preparation time:
5–8 minutes
Freezing:
Not recommended

1. Scoop the flesh from the melon using a melon baller, or cut into cubes. Place in a bowl and stir in the remaining ingredients.
2. Transfer to individual dishes to serve.

FILLED BRANDY SNAPS

3 bananas
2 teaspoons lemon juice
⅔ cup heavy cream,
whipped

1 tablespoon Greek
strained yogurt
8–12 brandy snaps

Serves 4–6
Preparation time:
5 minutes
Freezing:
Not recommended

1. Mash the bananas and mix with the lemon juice to prevent browning. Fold into the cream with the yogurt.
2. Spoon or pipe the mixture into the brandy snaps.

VARIATION
Replace the bananas with ½ cup mashed raspberries.

INSTANT ALTERNATIVES

These recipes are for those meal times—particularly breakfast—when you don't have time for or don't feel like eating but you know you need something to keep you going. They are as 'instant' as you can get—ready in less than 5 minutes—and are much better for you than cookies or potato chips.

FRUIT FLIP

Cream cheese lightened with lemon juice is delicious served with soft fruits.

*3/4 cup cream cheese
whipped with
3 tablespoons
lemon juice
7 oz can apricot halves in
fruit juice, drained*

*1 1/4 cups milk
1 teaspoon honey
(optional)
1 tablespoon chopped
roasted filberts to
decorate*

Serves 2
Preparation time:
4 minutes
Freezing:
Not recommended

1. Place all the ingredients in a blender or food processor and work until smooth; add the honey to taste, if you wish.
2. Pour into 2 glasses and sprinkle with the filberts.

VARIATION
Replace the apricots with 1/4 lb fresh strawberries.

COTTAGE CHEESE WITH FRUIT

This is a delicious summer lunchtime snack that looks pretty as well. Any combination of fruit can be used, e.g. apple quarters with sliced bananas and kiwi fruit. Use the fruit to scoop up the cottage cheese.

*1 slice watermelon, sliced
1/4 lb strawberries
1 nectarine or peach,
sliced*

*1/2 cup cottage cheese
mint sprig to garnish
(optional)*

Serves 1
Preparation time:
3 minutes
Freezing:
Not recommended

Arrange the fruit and cottage cheese on individual serving plates. Garnish with mint, if you wish, to serve.

PINEAPPLE AND PAPAYA COCKTAIL

15 oz can papaya cubes in
*   juice*
8 oz can pineapple pieces
*   in natural juice*
1 cup sour cream

1 tablespoon desiccated
*   coconut*
1 tablespoon white rum
*   (optional)*
TO SERVE (optional):
2 lime slices, halved

Serves 4
Preparation time:
2 minutes
Freezing:
Not recommended

1. Place all the ingredients in a blender or food processor and work until smooth.
2. Pour into 4 glasses, and decorate with lime slices if you wish.

VITALITY DRINK

First thing in the morning many of us don't feel like eating anything, although this is the time our bodies most need food to raise our blood sugar levels and give us energy. Try this drink instead—it's tasty and nutritious.

3/4 cup tropical fruit juice
1 egg
2 teaspoons wheatgerm

orange slice to decorate
*   (optional)*

Serves 1
Preparation time:
2 minutes
Freezing:
Not recommended

1. Place all the ingredients in a blender or food processor and work until smooth.
2. Pour into a tall glass, decorate with the orange slice, if you wish, and drink immediately.

BLACKBERRY AND APPLE YOGURT

15 oz can stewed apples
8 oz can blackberries in
*   fruit juice, drained,*
*   or 1/2 lb fresh blackberries*
1 cup Greek strained
*   yogurt*

pinch of ground
*   cinnamon*
1/2 cup slivered almonds
*   (optional)*

Serves 4
Preparation time:
3 minutes
Freezing:
Not recommended

Mix all the ingredients together and divide between individual dishes to serve.

HEALTH DRINK

The addition of wheatgerm is very beneficial. It provides
essential vitamins and other nutrients.

1 egg
2 bananas, chopped
roughly
1 tablespoon wheatgerm
²/₃ cup pineapple or
orange juice

1¼ cups plain yogurt
1–2 teaspoons honey
(optional)
TO SERVE:
1 tablespoon chopped
roasted filberts

1. Place all the ingredients in a blender or food processor
and work until smooth; add the honey to taste, if you wish.
2. Pour into 2 glasses, sprinkle with the nuts and serve
immediately.

Serves 2
Preparation time:
2 minutes
Freezing:
Not recommended

INDEX

Photography by: Clive Streeter
Designed by: Sue Storey
Home economist: Clare Gordon-Smith
Stylist: Alison Williams
Illustration by: Linda Smith
U.S. Consultant Editor: Carla Capalbo